DESSERTS

Cook Books from Amish Kitchens

Phyllis Pellman Good • Rachel Thomas Pellman

Good Books

Intercourse, PA 17534
800/762-7171
www.GoodBooks.com

DESSERTS
Cook Books from Amish Kitchens

Lighten up a meal with apple strudel or sunbeam tapioca! A refreshing dessert can be the right finish to any dinner. Sometimes graham cracker pudding. Sometimes apricot sponge.

Cover art and design by Cheryl A. Benner.
Design and art in body by Craig N. Heisey; Calligraphy by Gayle Smoker.
This special edition is an adaptation of *Desserts: From Amish and Mennonite Kitchens*, *Pennsylvania Dutch Cookbooks*, and from *Cook Books by Good Books*.

Contents

Apple Strudel

1½ cup flour   Makes 9-12 servings
½ cup sugar
⅛ tsp. salt
½ cup butter or margarine
5 cups apples, peeled and sliced
½ cup sugar
3 Tbsp. tapioca
⅔ tsp. cinnamon

1. Cut flour, ½ cup sugar, salt, and margarine together with two knives or a pastry cutter. Reserve ¾ cup crumb mixture for topping.
2. Press remaining crumb mixture on bottom and sides of 8" or 9" square pan.
3. Mix apples, ½ cup sugar, tapioca, and cinnamon and spread over crust.
4. Bake at 425° for 20 minutes. Sprinkle reserved crumbs an top and bake 20 minutes more.
5. Serve warm or cold with whipped cream or ice cream.

Apple Dumplings

8 apples, cored   Makes 8 servings
   and pared
3 cups flour
1 tsp. salt
1¼ cup shortening
1 egg, beaten
⅓ cup cold water
1 Tbsp. vinegar
½ cup margarine
1 cup brown sugar
4 Tbsp. water

1. Mix flour and salt. Cut in shortening.
2. Combine egg, ⅓ cup cold water, and vinegar and stir into the shortening mixture. Let stand a few minutes.
3. Roll out dough on a floured board and cut into squares, so that each is large enough to fit up around each apple. When an apple is completely wrapped in dough, place it in a greased 9"x13" baking pan.
4. Bring margarine, brown sugar, and 4 Tbsp. water to a boil. Pour over dumplings.
5. Bake at 350° for 40~50 minutes or until dumplings are golden brown.

Fruit Cobbler

1¼ cups flour, sifted   Makes 8 servings
1½ tsp. baking powder
½ tsp. salt
½ cup sugar
½ cup milk
2 Tbsp. shortening, melted
1¾ cup fruit
2 cups hot water or fruit juice
¾ cup sugar
2 Tbsp. margarine

1. Sift flour, baking powder, salt, and ½ cup sugar together. Add milk and shortening and stir only until smooth.
2. Spread dough evenly in greased shallow pan (about 12"x 8"). Arrange fruit over top.
3. Combine hot water or juice, ¾ cup sugar, and margarine in a saucepan and bring to a boil. Pour over fruit.
4. Bake immediately at 375° for 45~50 minutes. Serve warm.

Note:
Blueberries, peaches, cherries, or raspberries all work well in this cobbler.

Cherry Delight

2 cups graham
    cracker crumbs
½ cup butter
1 8 oz. package cream cheese, softened
2 cups whipped cream
¾ cup sugar
4½ Tbsp. cornstarch
3 cups water
2 cups cherries

Makes about 15 servings

1. Combine cracker crumbs and butter. Mix until crumbly. Reserve 1 cup for topping. Pat crumbs into 9"x13" pan. Bake at 350° for 5 minutes. Cool.
2. Beat cream cheese until fluffy. Add whipped cream. Spread mixture over crumb crust.
3. Combine sugar, cornstarch, and water. Cook over medium heat, stirring constantly, until mixture is thick and clear. Remove from heat. Stir in fruit. Spread fruit mixture over cream cheese. Sprinkle with reserved crumbs. Chill several hours before serving.

Plum Kuchen

½ cup sugar
1 cup butter or margarine
2 eggs
¼ tsp. cinnamon
⅛ tsp. cloves
1½ tsp. almond extract
½ Tbsp. lemon juice
2½ cups flour
1½ tsp. baking powder
½ cup ground almonds
2 lbs. plums (or apples or peaches)
    quartered
brown sugar
cinnamon
butter

Makes about
30 bars

1. Cream together sugar and butter. Add eggs and beat well. Stir in cinnamon, cloves, extract, and lemon juice.
2. Sift together flour and baking powder. Stir into sugar mixture. Stir in almonds. Chill dough for 1 hour. Press into a 9"x 13" baking pan or cookie sheet. Arrange fruit over dough in rows. Sprinkle with brown sugar and cinnamon. Dot with butter. Bake at 375° for 35 minutes.

Amish Date Pudding

1 cup dates, chopped   Makes about
1 cup boiling water   18 servings
1 tsp. baking soda
1 cup sugar
1 egg, beaten
3 Tbsp. butter, melted
1 cup flour
1 tsp. vanilla
½ cup nuts, chopped
3 cups sweetened whipped cream
3 bananas, sliced

1.   Combine dates, water, and soda. Mix well and let cool.
2.   Add remaining ingredients except cream and bananas and mix well.
3.   Pour batter into a greased, waxed paper lined 9"x13" pan. Bake at 350° for 30-40 minutes.
4.   Allow cake to cool. To serve, crumble cake slightly. Fold with whipped cream and sliced bananas.

Rhubarb Crunch

1 cup flour, sifted   Makes 6-8 servings
    (½ white; ½ whole wheat)
¼ cup oatmeal, uncooked
1 cup brown sugar, packed
½ cup butter, melted
1 tsp. cinnamon
1 cup sugar
2 Tbsp. cornstarch
1 cup water
1 tsp. vanilla
2 cups rhubarb, diced

1. Stir together flour, oatmeal, brown sugar, butter, and cinnamon until crumbly. Set aside half of crumbs. Pat remaining crumbs over bottom of 9" square baking pan.
2. Combine sugar, cornstarch, water, and vanilla, stirring until smooth. Add rhubarb and cook until mixture becomes thick and clear.
3. Pour rhubarb sauce over crumbs. Crumble remaining crumbs over top sauce.
4. Bake at 450° for 1 hour.

Variation:

Use cherries or blueberries instead of rhubarb.

Fruit Upside-down Pudding

2 cups brown sugar   Makes 8 servings
4 eggs
3 Tbsp. hot water
1 cup flour
1 tsp. baking powder
½ tsp. vanilla
3 Tbsp. butter
2 cups fruit, any kind

1. Combine 1 cup brown sugar and eggs. Beat well. Add water and beat again. Add flour, baking powder, and vanilla and mix well.
2. Combine remaining brown sugar and butter in heavy saucepan. Heat until sugar is melted. Pour caramel mixture into bottom of a 9"x9" cake pan. Add fruit. Spread batter over fruit. Bake at 350° for 30 minutes. Remove from oven and immediately turn pan upside down onto a serving platter. Serve warm with milk.

Peach Long Cake

        4 cups peaches,   Makes 10 servings
            sliced
        ½ cup sugar

Dough

        2 cups flour
        4 tsp. baking powder
        6 Tbsp. sugar
        ¾ tsp. salt
        ⅓ cup shortening
        1 large egg, beaten
        ⅔ cup milk

1. Sprinkle sugar over sliced peaches. Set aside.
2. Sift flour. Add baking powder, sugar, and salt. Cut in shortening. Add egg and milk and stir until moistened. Spread dough into a well-greased 9"x 13" pan. Arrange peach slices over dough.

Topping

        ¼ cup margarine
        ¼ cup sugar
        3 Tbsp. flour

1. Cream together all ingredients. Drop by spoonfuls over peaches.
2. Bake at 375° for 30 minutes. Serve warm with milk or whipped cream.

Apricot Sponge

1 lb. dried apricots
1 pkg. unflavored gelatin
   dissolved in ¼ cup cold water
2 cups apricot juice
1 cup sugar
juice of ½ lemon
2 egg whites
whipped cream

Makes about
12 servings

1. Place apricots in heavy saucepan and cover with water. Cook until soft. Drain apricots reserving juice. Add hot water to make 2 cups juice.
2. Mash apricots through vegetable press. Combine apricot pulp and juice, gelatin, sugar, and lemon juice in large mixing bowl. Beat until cold. Fold in slightly beaten egg whites. Pour into mold or serving dish. Chill. Serve with whipped cream.

Creamy Rice Pudding

1 quart milk   Makes 10 servings
½ cup rice
2 Tbsp. butter
¼ cup sugar
¼ tsp. salt
2 eggs
1 tsp. vanilla

1. Stir together milk, rice, butter, sugar, and salt. Pour into double boiler and cook slowly for 1-1½ hours until rice is soft.
2. Beat the eggs. Remove 1 cup hot milk and rice from double boiler and gradually add to the beaten eggs. Then add the egg mixture to the rest of the pudding. Stir in the vanilla. Serve either warm or cold.

Variations:
1. Add ¼-½ tsp. nutmeg to rice mixture before cooking.
2. After pudding cools, fold in ½ cup crushed pineapple or ½ cup banana slices, and 1 cup whipped cream.

Old-Fashioned Bread Pudding

5 slices bread, at
   least 3 days old
1 cup raisins, optional
3 cups milk
⅓ cup sugar
pinch of salt
3 eggs, slightly beaten
¼ tsp. cinnamon
2 Tbsp. sugar

Makes 10 servings

1. Toast bread lightly, butter generously, then break into pieces, about ¼" square. Arrange in buttered 9"x9" baking dish. Sprinkle with raisins.
2. Scald the milk. Stir in sugar and salt. Pour over eggs and blend thoroughly.
3. Pour over bread and stir so the bread is completely wet. Combine cinnamon and sugar and sprinkle over top.
4. Set baking dish in pan of hot water. Bake at 350° for 1 hour or until a knife, inserted in the center of the pudding, comes out clean. Serve hot or cold.

Egg Custard

4 eggs
½ cup sugar
¼ tsp. salt
1 tsp. vanilla
4 cups scalded milk

Makes about
7 servings

1. Combine all ingredients in blender and mix thoroughly. Pour into custard cups. Set cups in shallow baking pan and add hot water to cover all but ½" of the custard cups. Bake at 475° for 5 minutes and then 425° for 15-20 minutes or until set. Cool before serving.

Variations:

1. Sprinkle custards with nutmeg before baking.

2. Add ¾ cup coconut to custards before baking.

3. Add 2 cups mashed, cooked pumpkin, ½ tsp. ginger, 1 tsp. cinnamon, ½ tsp. cloves, ¼ tsp. nutmeg, and ¼ tsp. salt to custards before baking.

Cracker Pudding

2 eggs, separated   Makes 6-8 servings
⅔ cup sugar
1 quart milk
1¼-1½ cups saltine crackers,
    coarsely broken
¾ cup coconut, grated (optional)
1 tsp. vanilla
3 Tbsp. sugar

1. Beat egg yolks and sugar together. Pour into saucepan and heat. Gradually add the milk, stirring constantly.
2. Add crackers and coconut and cook until thickened. Remove from heat and stir in vanilla.
3. Pour into baking dish. Add 3 Tbsp. sugar to egg whites and beat untill stiffened. Spread over pudding, then brown the meringue under the broiler.

"This is very easy and quick to make—and has a good consistency."

Graham Cracker Pudding

16 whole Graham crackers
¼ cup sugar
¼ cup butter
4 tsp. flour
½ cup plus 2 Tbsp. sugar
2 cups milk
3 eggs, separated
½ tsp. vanilla
1 cup shredded coconut

Makes about 9 servings

1. Crush graham crackers. Combine with ¼ cup sugar and butter. Mix to form fine crumbs. Press ¾ of crumb mixture into bottom and sides of baking dish. Reserve remaining crumbs.
2. Combine flour and ½ cup sugar in top of double boiler. Add milk. Heat to boiling. Beat egg yolks and combine with ½ cup hot milk mixture. Pour this into remaining hot milk and heat to boiling again. Boil 2-3 minutes, stirring constantly. Remove from heat and add vanilla and coconut. Pour into cracker-lined dish.

3. Beat egg whites until stiff. Gradually add remaining 2 Tbsp. sugar. Pile beaten egg whites on top of pudding. Sprinkle with reserved cracker crumbs. Bake at 350° for 5-8 minutes until meringue is browned. Cool before serving.

Sunbeam Tapioca

½ cup sugar   Makes 6 servings
¼ cup quick cooking tapioca
½ tsp. salt
½ cup pineapple juice
1 cup water
½ cup orange juice
1½ Tbsp. lemon juice
½ cup diced orange sections
1 cup crushed pineapple, drained

1. In heavy saucepan combine sugar, tapioca, salt, pineapple juice, and water. Bring to a boil. Boil 3-5 minutes until thickened. Cool.
2. Stir in remaining ingredients. Chill. Serve with whipped cream.

Tapioca Pudding

4 cups milk
⅓ cup minute tapioca
2 eggs, separated
½ cup sugar
pinch of salt
½ tsp. vanilla or lemon extract

Makes about
10 servings

1.   Combine milk and tapioca in heavy saucepan. Cook, stirring constantly, until tapioca is clear.
2.   Beat egg yolks with sugar and salt. Add ½ cup hot milk mixture to egg yolks. Return this to remaining hot milk. Heat again to boiling point. Boil 2 minutes, stirring constantly. Remove from heat. Fold in stiffly beaten egg whites and flavoring. Pour into serving dish.

Variation:
   1. Substitute ¼ cup honey in place of sugar.
   2. Use 3 cups grape juice and 1 cup milk instead of 4 cups milk.

Spanish Cream

1 envelope unflavored   Makes 6-8 servings
   gelatin
2 Tbsp. sugar
⅛ tsp. salt
2 eggs, separated
2 cups milk
1 tsp. vanilla
4 Tbsp. sugar

1. Mix gelatin, 2 Tbsp. sugar, and salt thoroughly in top of double boiler.
2. Beat egg yolks and milk together and add to gelatin. Cook over boiling water, about 5 minutes, until gelatin dissolves.
3. Remove from heat and stir in the vanilla.
4. Beat egg whites until stiff, adding the 4 Tbsp. sugar while beating.
5. Fold stiff whites into pudding. Pour in serving dish and chill until set. (The pudding will separate into 2 layers.) Serve topped with whipped cream.

Vanilla Pudding

1 cup milk   Makes 18-20 servings
2 cups sugar
4 eggs, beaten
3 rounded Tbsp. cornstarch
1 rounded Tbsp. flour
pinch of salt
2 Tbsp. vanilla
1¾ quarts milk

1. Mix together 1 cup milk, sugar, eggs, cornstarch, flour, and salt until smooth.
2. Add to remaining milk and vanilla. Slowly heat to the boiling point.
3. Remove from heat and cool.

Cottage Steam Pudding

1 cup sugar   Makes 8 servings
3 Tbsp. butter, melted
1 egg
2 cups flour
1 tsp. soda
2 tsp. cream of tartar
1 cup milk
1 cup raisins or other fruit

1. Cream sugar and butter. Add egg and beat well. Add dry ingredients and milk. Beat thoroughly. Stir in fruit.
2. Place in double boiler. Steam 1½-1¾ hours. Do not lift lid any time during steaming. Remove from kettle onto serving platter. Serve warm with milk.

Grapenut Pudding

1 Tbsp. margarine, melted   Makes 6 servings
½ cup sugar
2 egg yolks
1½ cups milk
½ cup raisins
¾ cup grapenuts
2 egg whites
1 tsp. vanilla

1. Mix together the margarine, sugar, egg yolks, milk, raisins, and grapenuts.
2. Pour into a greased casserole and bake at 350° for 45 minutes or until browned.
3. Beat egg whites until soft peaks form. Fold into pudding along with vanilla.
4. Cool. Serve with a dollop of whipped cream.

Snow Pudding

1 cup water   Makes 6 servings
6 Tbsp. sugar
3½ Tbsp. cornstarch
2 egg whites
1 tsp. vanilla
1½ cup milk
2 egg yolks, beaten

1. Combine water, 3 Tbsp. sugar, and 2 Tbsp. cornstarch in heavy saucepan. Cook until thickened.
2. Beat egg whites until stiff. Stir into hot cornstarch mixture. Add ½ tsp. vanilla. Pour mixture into serving dish.
3. Combine milk, egg yolks, remaining sugar, cornstarch, and vanilla. Cook over medium heat until thickened. Pour over first layer in serving dish. Cool. Serve with whipped cream if desired.

Frozen Pumpkin Parfait Squares

1½ cups graham   Makes 9-12 servings
     cracker crumbs
¼ cup butter or margarine, melted

¼ cup sugar
½ cup pecans, finely chopped
1 qt. vanilla ice cream
1½ cup pumpkin, mashed
½ cup brown sugar
½ tsp. salt
1 tsp. cinnamon
¼ tsp. ginger
⅓ tsp. ground cloves
whipping cream
chopped pecans

1. Combine crumbs, butter, sugar, and chopped nuts. Press mixture firmly against bottom and sides of 9" square pan. Bake at 375° for 8 minutes. Cool.
2. Allow ice cream to soften until it becomes custardy. Stir in pumpkin, brown sugar, and spices.
3. Pile into cooled crust. Place in freezer until hard. Cover with foil to store.
4. Take from freezer 20 minutes before serving; then cut into squares.
5. Dollop with whipped cream and sprinkle with chopped nuts.

Scotch Refrigerator Dish

3 Tbsp. margarine   Makes 12 servings
1 cup light brown sugar
¼ cup flour
1½ cups milk
2 eggs, separated
1 box vanilla wafers, crushed
1 cup pecans, coarsely chopped

1. Melt margarine over water in top of double boiler. Mix brown sugar and flour and add to melted margarine. Blend well.
2. Add milk slowly. Cook over hot water, stirring constantly until it becomes thick and smooth. Cook 15 minutes longer.
3. Slowly add slightly beaten egg yolks. Cook for 2 minutes. Remove from heat and gently fold in stiffly beaten egg whites.
4. Cover bottom of 9"x 9" baking pan with ½ of cookie crumbs. Cover with ½ of cooked filling. Top with ⅓ of cookie crumbs and ½ the pecans. Pour in remaining filling. Top with rest of cookie crumbs and pecans. Chill several hours. Top with whipped cream to serve.

Zucchini Bars

¾ cup butter or
    margarine
½ cup brown sugar
½ cup granulated sugar
2 eggs
1 tsp. vanilla
1¾ cup flour
1½ tsp. baking powder
1 cup shredded coconut
2 cups shredded zucchini
½ cup nuts, chopped

Makes about
2 doz. bars

1. Beat butter until light and fluffy. Gradually beat in sugar. Add eggs and beat well. Add vanilla.
2. Sift together flour and baking powder. Stir into egg mixture. Stir in zucchini, coconut, and nuts. Spread evenly in well greased 10"x15"x1½" pan. Bake at 350° for 40 minutes. Cool. Cut in bars.

Variation:
    Frost with butter cream frosting flavored with a bit of cinnamon and vanilla.

Peanut Butter Bars

¼ cup butter or margarine, melted
Makes 48 bars
1¼ cups flour
½ cup brown sugar
1 cup peanut butter
6 oz. chocolate bits
3 Tbsp. water

1. Blend butter, flour, and sugar and press into a 13" x 9" x 2" baking pan. Bake 20 minutes at 350°.
2. Spread peanut butter over above mixture. Cool.
3. Melt chocolate bits and water. Spread over peanut butter. Cool. Cut into bars.

Hello Dollies

¼ cup butter or margarine
Makes about 2 dozen squares
1 cup graham cracker crumbs
1 cup coconut
1 cup chocolate bits
1 cup pecans, chopped
1 can sweetened condensed milk

1. Spread softened butter on bottom of a 9"x 9" baking pan.
2. Add cracker crumbs, then coconut, then chocolate bits, then pecans. Pour milk over all. Bake at 325° for 30 minutes. Cool and cut in squares.

Butterscotch Bars

½ cup butter or margarine
2 cups brown sugar
2 cups flour
1 tsp. salt
2 tsp. baking powder
2 eggs
1 tsp. vanilla
1 cup peanuts, chopped

Makes 1 long cake pan

1. Melt butter, then stir in brown sugar, and set aside to cool.
2. Mix together the flour, salt, and baking powder.
3. Stir eggs into cooled brown sugar mixture, then blend in dry ingredients, vanilla, and peanuts.
4. Spread in a greased 9"x 13" cake pan. Bake at 350° for 30 minutes.

Cottage Cheese Cake

1½ cups cornflakes,   Makes 9-12 servings
   finely crushed
¼ cup sugar
1 tsp. cinnamon
¼ tsp. nutmeg
¼ cup margarine or butter, melted
¾ cup sugar
2 envelopes (2 Tbsp) unflavored gelatin
¼ tsp. salt
2 egg yolks, beaten
1 6 oz. can (¾ cup) evaporated milk
1 tsp. lemon peel, grated
24 oz. cottage cheese, sieved or blended
1 Tbsp. lemon juice
1½ tsp. vanilla
2 egg whites
¼ cup sugar
½ to 1 cup whipped cream

1. Combine cornflakes, ¼ cup sugar, cinna-mon, nutmeg, and margarine to form crust. Reserve ⅓ of mixture. Press remaining crumbs on bottom of 9" square baking pan. Chill.
2. In double boiler combine ¾ cup sugar, gelatin, and salt. Stir in egg yolks and

milk. Cook over simmering water, stirring until gelatin dissolves and mixture thickens. Remove from heat.

3. Stir lemon peel, cottage cheese, lemon juice, and vanilla into gelatin mixture. Chill until partially congealed and custardy.

4. Beat egg whites until soft peaks form. Gradually add ¼ cup sugar and beat until stiff peaks form. Fold into gelatin mixture.

5. Fold in whipped cream. Pour over corn-flake crust. Sprinkle with remaining crumbs and chill.

"This cake works well any time. It looks cool for summer and snowy white for winter holidays."

Ice Cream

3 eggs, beaten   Makes 4 quarts
2 cups sugar
3 cups cream
2 tsp. vanilla
dash of salt
1 quart fruit, chopped

1. Mix all ingredients together thoroughly. Pour into 4 quart freezer container, adding additional fruit or cream if necessary to make container ⅔ full.
2. Turn freezer until firm.

"We make this on family evenings after the work is done, or on any other occasion we can come up with!"